The Ideas into Action Series draws on the practical
knowledge that the Center for Creative Leadership
(CCL), since its inception in 1970, has generated
through its research and educational activities
conducted in partnership with hundreds of thousands
of leaders. Much of this knowledge is shared—in a way
that is distinct from the typical university department,
professional association, or consultancy. CCL is not
simply a collection of individual experts, although
the individual credentials of its staff are impressive;
rather it is a community, with its members holding
certain principles in common and working together
to understand and generate practical responses to
today's leadership and organizational challenges. The
purpose of the series is to provide leaders with specific
advice on how to complete a developmental task or
solve a leadership challenge. In doing that, the series
carries out CCL's mission to advance the understanding,
practice, and development of leadership for the benefit
of society worldwide. We think you will find the Ideas
into Action Series an important addition to your
leadership toolkit.

CCL is sincerely grateful to **Michael H. Hoppe**, who served as lead contributor on the first edition of *Active Listening*, published in 2006.

Special thanks to Craig Chappelow and Andre Keil for reviewing an early version of this work.

ACTIVE
LISTENING

Improve Your Ability to Listen and Lead

———— **Second Edition** ————

First edition published 2006.

Second edition 2019.

978-1-60491-936-3 – Print

978-1-60491-937-0 – Ebook

CCL. No.00471

Cataloging-in-publication data on file with the Library of Congress.

Published by Center for Creative Leadership
CCL Press

Manager, Publication Development: Peter Scisco
Editor: Shaun Martin
Rights and Permissions: Kelly Lombardino
   https://www.ccl.org/permission-republish-request/

Design and Layout: Carly Bell

CONTENTS

LISTENING AND LEADERSHIP

Maria is a smart, successful leader and a likeable coworker. Six months ago, she took on a role with greater responsibility in a new division. To her surprise, she's having difficulty leading this new group. She is unable to pinpoint the reason for the friction between herself and several of her direct reports, and she's frustrated that her new group hasn't jelled. She calls one of her direct reports in to address the issue. Here's how it goes:

MARIA (as Jim enters her office): Hi, Jim. Thanks for taking a few minutes to talk to me; I really appreciate it. I've been sensing some tension among the members of the team, like something isn't working as well as it should, and I wanted to talk to you about it.

JIM (unsure where to start): Well... I feel like if there were a bit more, um, flexibility—I think that would make a difference.

MARIA (looking a little surprised): Flexibility? What do you mean?

JIM: Like, in our schedules—say, to take a shorter lunch, and then leave a little earlier in the evening.

MARIA (still clearly feeling confused): Oh... okay. I guess I don't see how that can help the tension thing?

JIM: Right, yeah. So, in my case, I have to get to my son's day care after work no later than 5:20; otherwise the day care providers end up angry—and they charge a dollar every minute I'm late. If my work runs over at all and traffic isn't perfect, it gets super stressful. So I'm watching the clock constantly to get out right on time. And it basically kills the last hour and a half of my productivity.

MARIA (raising an eyebrow): So, you want to shave off some time at the end of the day so your kid's day care won't charge you so much.

JIM (searching for the right words): Well, no... not "shave time" off the workday—

MARIA: But, Jim, isn't that what you just told me? That you wanted to leave a little early, for personal reasons?

JIM (getting flustered): Well, no—I mean, yes, I did say that, but—

MARIA: Jim, do you know that I was assigned to lead this team in order to "straighten out" some things? I mean, we clearly have a great team, but the numbers show it's gotten tired lately and needs refocusing. And granting this kind of personal request would put me in a real bind—

JIM: Yes, but—

MARIA (with a hint of sternness): Jim, look, I'm sorry. I know this is important to you—a dollar a minute is a lot of money—but if I make an exception for you, I'll have to make exceptions for everyone. And right now, what we need is more focus and unity in the team, not less.

MARIA (after a moment of uncomfortable silence): Jim, I really am sorry. But you understand, don't you?

JIM (pursing his lips slightly): Yes, Maria. I understand. I'll work on keeping my focus on the job.

MARIA: Good. I know that's what we need right now—to focus on getting the team back on its "A game."

MARIA (after another uncomfortable pause): So, um... did you have any other thoughts about that?

JIM: No. I think that's everything.

MARIA (rising to see Jim out of the room): Great! I'm really glad we had this chance to talk. We've got a really great team—I know we'll get this turned around in no time. In the meantime, if anything else occurs to you, my door is always open.

JIM (after a brief pause): Sure.

Fortunately, most leaders do better than Maria. But, like her, many overestimate their ability to listen to others. They are often surprised to find out that their peers, direct reports, or bosses think they don't listen well and are impatient, judgmental, arrogant, or unaware.

Assessments of thousands of leaders in CCL's database indicate that many leaders have development needs that directly relate to their listening skills:

- dealing with people's feelings

- accepting criticism well

- trying to understand what other people think before making judgments about them

- encouraging direct reports to share

- using feedback to make necessary changes in their behavior

- being open to the input of others

- putting themselves in another person's shoes and imagining that person's point of view

The ability to listen—to really understand what someone else is trying to communicate—fundamentally affects your ability to lead. Most leaders understand this, at least on a theoretical level. However, although they may have the best intentions, they may not see the need to develop these skills (or they think they're already good listeners) and

Impact of Poor Listening

Colleagues, direct reports, and others often describe poor listeners in these ways:

- He's not really interested in what I have to say.

- She's already made up her mind. Why does she bother to ask what we think?

- He's critical of everyone. No one wants to speak up only to be shot down.

- She's just really hard to talk to.

- He only listens to certain people.

- She's arrogant.

- He doesn't pay attention to what's going on under the surface.

- I can't get through a sentence without her interrupting.

don't always know specifically what to do or avoid doing to become better listeners. By learning the skills and behaviors of active listening, you can become a more effective leader. You can use active listening with direct reports, peers, customers, bosses, stakeholders, and others to:

- hear accurately

- understand

- draw out ideas and information

- empathize

- gather information

- show respect

- build self-esteem

- find answers

- show appreciation

- buy time

- connect

- question assumptions and ideas

- weigh options

- change perspectives

- soothe or heal

- set the stage for something else

- build relationships

Have you thought about how well you listen to others and what effect your listening skills have on your ability to communicate, to coach, to help others develop their talents—to lead well? You can take a quick measure of where you stand using the "Assess Your Listening Skills" worksheet below.

Assess Your Listening Skills

To assess how well you listen to others, rate yourself on the following behaviors. Use a five-point scale:

1	2	3	4	5
almost never	rarely	sometimes	often	almost always

When I listen to others:

1.____ I sit behind my desk, accept phone calls, shuffle papers, use my smartphone, or otherwise communicate by my activities or gestures that I am not fully attentive.

2.____ I have a hard time concentrating on what is being said.

3.____ I am annoyed when someone slows me down.

4.____ I think about what I want to say next rather than about what the other person is saying.

5.____ I don't like it when someone questions my ideas or actions.

6.____ I interrupt or show signs of impatience as I wait for the other person to finish talking.

7.____ I give advice too soon; I suggest courses of action or solutions to problems before the other person has fully explained his or her perspective.

8.____ I tell people not to feel the way they do.

9.____ I sense that people seem upset after talking to me.

10.____ I tend to talk significantly more than the other person talks.

11.____ I make it a point to fill any silences.

12.____ I am uncomfortable or at a loss when the other person expresses emotions.

13.____ I have a hard time understanding what people are trying to say.

14. _____ I avoid asking any questions that would encourage the other person to talk more.

15. _____ I ask questions for which I already have the answers.

16. _____ I expect yes or no answers.

17. _____ I frequently lose track of where the conversation is going.

18. _____ I have a hard time remembering what has been said when a conversation is over.

19. _____ I frequently discover that things the other person and I have agreed upon during a conversation don't get done.

20. _____ I avoid repeating things or letting the other person repeat things.

21. _____ I keep my thoughts to myself.

22._____ I keep my feelings to myself.

23._____ I avoid sharing personal experiences.

24._____ I try hard not to let the other person know how his or her behavior during the conversation affects me.

Keep track of any items where you gave yourself a 4 or 5, as those areas represent where your active listening skills may be lacking. We'll revisit this assessment further along in this book.

THE ACTIVE LISTENING SKILL SET

Active listening refers to your willingness and ability to hear and understand. Many of us intuitively know what active listening looks, sounds, and feels like. However, we may not know what we need to do to be seen as good listeners. Leaders who practice active listening are able to draw out more information—and information that's more meaningful—during a conversation. At its most engaging and effective, active listening is the norm for conversation, and everyone involved is a full participant. It involves bringing about and finding common ground, connecting to each other, and opening up to new possibilities.

Active listening involves six skills: paying attention, suspending judgment, reflecting, clarifying, summarizing, and sharing. Each skill contributes to the active listening mindset, and each skill includes various techniques or behaviors, but these skills are not mutually exclusive.

For example, paying attention isn't something you stop doing when you start suspending judgment. And the skills aren't consistently weighted in importance, either. In one conversation, clarifying may take much effort and time; in another conversation, gaining clarity and understanding may be quick and easy.

Active Listening Skill Set

Pay Attention

A primary goal of active listening is to set a comfortable tone and allow time and opportunity for the other person to think and speak. By paying attention to your behavior and that of the other person, you create the setting for productive dialogue. Pay attention to the following:

Your frame of mind. Get in the frame of mind of a listener and learner. Your intention is to connect to and understand—not interrogate—the other person. Operate from a place of deep respect, letting yourself empathize with the other person. Be comfortable being silent. You'll need to accurately summarize the other person's ideas, concerns, and feelings at the end of the discussion, so prepare to do so—take notes and ask clarifying questions.

Your body language. Maintain comfortable eye contact. Show interest. Lean forward. Maintain open body position and posture. Give nonverbal affirmations. For example, nod to show that you understand. Smile at appropriate moments. Indicate that you understand and allow the other person to keep talking.

The other person. Observing and understanding accurately require careful attention. Pay close attention to the other person's nonverbal and verbal behavior in order to pick up on the important information that it offers and to make sense of it. There are often cues that convey the type of emotion that underlies the perspective the other person is expressing. Listen for and pay attention to the tone, intensity, and loudness of voice, as well as facial expressions and physical posture. Watch for shifts in body language and voice. By focusing on the other person and being present in the moment, you convey that your primary purpose is to understand his or her point of view.

Suspend Judgment

Active listening requires an open mind—the willingness to hear ideas, accept different perspectives, and entertain new possibilities. Even when good listeners have strong views, they suspend judgment, hold their criticism, and avoid arguing or selling their point of view right away. Tell yourself, "I'm here to understand how the other person sees the world. Now is not the time to judge or give my view."

Suspending judgment is particularly important when tensions run high. Let the other person vent or blow off steam if needed. Don't jump immediately to problem-solving or to offering advice. Be comfortable not talking. Your main job is to listen and pay attention. This does

> **❝ I'm here to understand how the other person sees the world. Now is not the time to judge or give my view. ❞**

not mean that you agree; it shows that you are trying to understand.

Practice empathy. Empathy is the ability to put yourself in someone else's shoes, to temporarily live in that person's world without making any judgments about the situation. Demonstrating empathy is the behavior that expresses your willingness to understand the other person's situation. For example, if you say, "I'd be excited too if I had such attractive options before me", or "It must be really hard to make this choice," it helps you convey respect for the other person and his or her views and experiences.

Demonstrate an open mind. Show your intention to be open minded by saying something like "I have a different perspective, and I want to understand your view", or "My goal here is to understand, not to judge or make a decision."

Acknowledge differences. Each person brings a unique perspective to a situation. Experiences, cultures, personal backgrounds, and current circumstances all contribute to the way people react to one another. Communicate that you'd like to understand things from the other person's unique viewpoint.

Be patient. Slow down. Try to relax. Allow the other person to talk and elaborate. Don't speed the conversation along; allow pauses. Be comfortable with silence.

Reflect

Like a mirror, reflect information and emotions without

agreeing or disagreeing. Use paraphrasing—a brief, periodic recap of the other person's key points—to confirm your understanding. Reflecting the other person's information, perspective, and feelings is a way to indicate that you hear and understand. Don't assume that you understand correctly or that the other person knows you've heard; be explicit in stating what you understand the other person is telling you. By reflecting the other person's message and feelings, you create strong rapport and deepen the experience of collaborative exploration.

Paraphrase information. Demonstrate that you are tracking with the information presented by periodically restating the other person's basic ideas, emphasizing the facts. Responses such as "What I'm hearing is..." and "Let me make sure I understand what you're saying..." allow you to identify any disconnects and signal to the other person that you are getting it.

Paraphrase emotion. Identifying the feeling message that accompanies the content is equally important but often more challenging. Yet reflecting the other person's emotions is an effective way to get to the core of the issue. The feeling message may be contained in the words used, the tone of voice, the body language, or a combination of all these things. Using this technique shows the other person that you are paying close attention and that you are putting energy into understanding what he or she is communicating to you.

It may also help others by providing clarity about feelings they are experiencing but aren't consciously aware of. Here are some examples of paraphrasing emotion:

- You seem to have doubts about...

- It seems to me that you are feeling very happy about...

- It sounds as if you're feeling pretty frustrated and stuck.

Clarify

Double-check any issue that is ambiguous or unclear to you. Open-ended, clarifying, and probing questions, when used effectively, are important tools.

Open-ended questions. These questions draw people out and help them expand their ideas, and they allow you to uncover hidden issues. They also encourage people to reflect, rather than justify or defend a position or try to guess the "right" answer. Open-ended questions can't be answered with a simple yes or no. For example:

- What are your thoughts on...?

- What led you to draw this conclusion?

- What might happen next?

Clarifying questions. These questions help ensure understanding and clear up confusion. They define problems, uncover gaps in information, and encourage accuracy and precision. Any who, what, where, when, how, or why question can be a clarifying question, but those are not the only possibilities. For example:

- Let me see if I'm clear. Are you talking about...?

- I must have missed something. Could you repeat that?

- I am not sure that I got what you were saying. Can you explain it again another way?

Probing questions. These questions introduce new ideas or suggestions. Often they highlight details and contain an element of challenge. By asking probing questions, you invite reflection and a thoughtful response instead of telling others what to do. In answering probing questions, the other person takes on ownership of decisions and outcomes and can develop their problem-solving capacity. Examples of probing questions include the following:

- More specifically, what are some of the things you've tried?

- How direct have you been with your team about the consequences for the sales force if the situation doesn't change?

- What is it in your own leadership approach that might be contributing to your direct reports' failure to meet deadlines?

Summarize

To summarize is to briefly restate core themes raised by the other person during your conversation. Summarizing helps people identify those themes, and it confirms and solidifies your grasp of their perspectives and positions. A summary does not necessarily imply agreement or disagreement, but it may lead to additional questions as a transition to problem-solving. It also helps both parties to be clear on mutual responsibilities and follow up.

- These seem to be the key points you have expressed...

- What have you heard so far?

- To make sure we're on the same page, would you please summarize for both of us the key plans we've agreed upon today?

Share

Being an active listener doesn't mean being a sponge, passively soaking up the information coming your way. Active listening is first about understanding the other person, then about being understood, which is hard for anyone to learn and apply. It may be especially hard for people in leadership roles, who may have preconceptions about leaders as needing to be understood first so that others can follow.

When you have gained a clearer understanding of the other person's perspective, it's time to introduce your ideas, feelings, and suggestions and to address any concerns. Share your view and collaborate on solutions and next steps. For example:

- You're telling me that triggered the thought that...

- I'm relieved I wasn't the only one feeling that way.

- May I share something similar?

BARRIERS
TO ACTIVE
LISTENING

Most people would see some of the skills and behaviors associated with active listening as basic courtesy (not interrupting, for example). But other active listening skills (such as asking clarifying questions) are less familiar and may require instruction and practice. Leaders who seek to improve their active listening skills may face a number of barriers.

The Image of Leadership

The role of listening may contradict common cultural notions of what a leader is. In a society that values leaders who are action-oriented, charismatic, visionary, and directive, the expectation is that leaders should have the answers, call the shots, and do all the talking. This emphasis on the performance of leaders cuts into their ability to be quiet and listen.

Silence as Agreement

Listening quietly can sometimes be confused with agreement or acceptance of the other person's ideas and perspectives. When leaders disagree or have additional ideas and information, they may be quick to debate or respond. Active listening allows different viewpoints to be aired and assessed. It does not require you to discount or hold back your own opinion or objections; however, it does require allowing sufficient time to learn, uncover assumptions, and seek clarity—to listen with an open mind.

External Pressures

Contemporary organizations often operate in uncertain and complex environments, which makes it tempting not to listen. The daily demands placed on leaders make it difficult to slow down, focus, inquire, and listen. At the same time, one of the critical skills for dealing with uncertain conditions is to actively solicit information and make sense of it. Communicating effectively—especially the listening aspect— is a survival skill.

Lack of Know-How

Listening is a neglected communication skill. Much of the emphasis on communication by leaders is about how to effectively "get your message out." Less effort is made to ensure that leaders accurately receive the messages of others.

Individual Makeup

An individual's experience (being accustomed to working collaboratively or independently, for example) and personality (such as being action-driven, impatient, talkative, or reserved) may also create barriers to effective active listening.

Emotion

When people express strong feelings, it may be tempting to react quickly or passionately. It's better to use active listening to ease tensions, address conflict, and find common ground for solving problems. Subtler emotions, too, can make it difficult to listen well. When a leader is negotiating with someone he or she doesn't entirely respect, it may be a particular challenge to listen without judging, to be patient, and so on. Emotions are always going to play a role at work, but a good leader is able to manage his or her feelings and help others manage theirs.

Cultural Differences

The way we work, communicate, and lead is deeply connected to our cultural backgrounds. Routine or natural behaviors can be misinterpreted and can create unexpected problems when you are working with people whose cultural backgrounds are different from yours. Similarly, ideas and techniques that leaders learn—including techniques of active listening—have some level of cultural bias. While active listening may allow you to better communicate in culturally diverse settings, it is important to be mindful of your own assumptions and interpretations.

Communication Styles: Some Cultural Differences to Be Aware of

Cultural differences in conveying the message:

- Focus is on the words spoken: Nordic and Germanic Europe

- Focus is on how they are said: Asia and the Middle East

Cultural differences in pauses in conversation:

- Favor short pauses: Greece, Spain, Italy

- Favor medium-length pauses: Northern (non-Nordic) Europe and the USA

- Favor long pauses: Japan, Nordic countries

Cultural differences in the purpose of conversation:

- Achieving understanding: Australia, the USA, Germany, France, the Netherlands

- Achieving agreement and preserving relationships: Most Middle Eastern and Asian cultures

ACTIVE LISTENING AND VIRTUAL COMMUNICATION

Human beings are hardwired for in-person, face-to-face communication, with a vast quantity of information communicated nonverbally through subtle cues of posture, facial expression, and tone of voice. Shared history, assumptions, and social identity also ensure mutual understanding. Active listening, at its best, is the art of leveraging these cues and common background to create a safe space for drawing out information that may be both disconfirming and emotionally charged. But how does this play out in virtual communication?

While technology has in some ways made communication easy and instantaneous, it has also stripped communication of some of its richness and context. This presents a special set of problems for a leader who may rarely interact face-to-face with some (or all) of his or her supervisors, peers, or direct reports. Where the natural richness of in-person business relationships is lacking, individuals tend to fill in the gaps with assumptions, criticize coworkers more harshly, and interpret communication in a more negative light. The environment of trust—foundational to candid sharing of information—is harder to build and easier to tear down.

A leader who understands how these realities heighten both the need and the difficulty of active listening—and how to respond accordingly—has a crucial advantage over one who does not.

Creating a Foundation for Virtual Active Listening

Perhaps even more so than in the case of in-person active listening, it is incredibly important to set the groundwork for effective remote active listening before it's needed. When done well, this can help to mimic the benefits that underlie in-person communication, such as a stronger sense of common purpose and shared social identity, and more positive (or at least more accurate) assumptions about the deeper meaning or intent behind the words used.

Arrange a good introduction. One of the crucial aspects of active listening is the ability to create a space of empathy, which is inherently personal in nature. Any important virtual working relationship should, early on, involve an introduction designed to establish the humanness of the other person. This will help create some of the interpersonal rapport and social bonding that is lost when you don't share a workspace with a colleague. Depending on your situation, one or more of the following might be an option:

- Exchange photos and biographies that communicate something of your quirks, character, and philosophy of work to each other.

- Arrange a quasi-informal "get to know you" call via telephone or video conferencing and allow your conversation to stray beyond the confines of the project at hand.

- If the relationship has a lot at stake (e.g., a high-value project or a long series of smaller ones depends on it), consider investing in traveling for an initial face-to-face meeting.

Take special care regarding culture. Separately, cultural differences and virtual communications technology tend to complicate effective interpersonal communication.

Combined, they exacerbate each other—especially when one or both individuals do not have a strong understanding of the other's culture. If you are working extensively on a remote basis with people from a culture foreign to you, you should seriously consider investing time and energy in developing a deep awareness and appreciation of that culture so that when you listen, you truly grasp what they are telling you.

Cultivate a culture of listening and sharing. One of the great advantages of virtual collaboration is the ability to "push" large amounts of information out to many people at once. However, if the only communication between yourself and a coworker is this impersonal kind of information, initiating the kind of dialogue needed for active listening may come across as forced or unnatural. It is helpful from this perspective to keep a less formal line of communication open—a forum, instant messaging, or other social media platforms, for example—where you can seek real-time feedback or even appropriately discuss subjects of mutual interest that may not be directly project related. Use this to create opportunities to establish yourself as an interested audience who handles diverse views with candor and tact and respects others, not just as colleagues, but as people.

Tips for Active Listening in Virtual Settings

Exactly the same principles that lead to positive active listening outcomes in person apply in a virtual setting. However, because missing cues, sparser interpersonal interaction, and cultural differences make it more difficult to intuitively recognize virtual active listening opportunities, it is crucial that you be more systematic and more frequent in applying these principles.

- Resist the urge to multitask while having a conversation across technology, as this will distract you from catching cues.

- Learn to distinguish between information-pushing tasks and active listening tasks (usually tasks involving sensitive and potentially emotional human issues, such as resolving a seeming dysfunction within a team or gathering information for a performance review).

- Take greater note, especially in writing, of comments that seem strange or out of place, or that vaguely raise a yellow flag in your head; give yourself permission to ask about these comments, as they may represent the "tip of the iceberg" of an issue that is outside your experience or that you might otherwise miss.

- When an opportunity for active listening around a sensitive issue is discovered in a group setting, it is often appropriate to move that part of the conversation from a group setting (like email or a project board) to a richer, more exclusive setting (a personal phone call or video chat).

- Finally, be more deliberate and more frequent about applying the strategies mentioned in the Active Listening Skill Set—especially suspending judgment, reflecting, clarifying, and summarizing.

HOW TO IMPROVE YOUR ACTIVE LISTENING SKILLS

There are specific tips and activities you can use to practice and hone your active listening skills. Look back at the "Assess Your Listening Skills" exercise you completed earlier. If you gave yourself a 4 or 5 on any item, find that item below. We've listed tips for addressing each one; feel free to add ideas of your own. Then use our suggestions and your ideas to set goals and practice plans.

1. **I sit behind my desk, accept phone calls, shuffle papers...**

   - Select a place and time that will make distractions and disruptions less likely.

   - Ask others not to disturb you.

   - If you are in the middle of something important, ask the other person for a few minutes to complete your task. Then pay full attention to him or her.

2. **I have a hard time concentrating on what is being said.**

  - Turn toward the other person, make eye contact, and remove things in front of you that may distract you.

  - With permission from the other person, take notes to help you remember important points.

  - If a session gets long, suggest a short break.

3. **I am annoyed when someone slows me down.**

  - Consider the potential costs of not slowing down and listening to the other person.

  - Offer the other person a specified amount of time during which you will be fully attentive. If the conversation is not finished by then, suggest another time to continue.

  - Be proactive. Make room on your calendar every day to walk around and visit with people. Let them know you want to hear their concerns, suggestions, and needs.

4. **I think about what I want to say next rather than listen to the other person.**

   - Set a goal of being able to repeat the last sentence the other person says.

   - Allow yourself time to formulate your response after the other person finishes speaking.

   - Remind yourself that your primary goal as a listener is to understand, not to fix.

5. **I don't like it when someone questions my ideas or actions.**

   - Ask yourself why you think that your ideas and actions can't be improved upon.

   - Ask someone you trust to give you feedback if you have heard that you come across as a know-it-all.

   - Pay attention to your body language, tone of voice, facial expressions, and gestures when you're questioned.

6. I interrupt or show signs of impatience...

- Focus on what is being said, not what you want to say.

- Give the other person permission to call you out for interrupting him or her.

- Allow yourself time to formulate your response after the other person finishes speaking.

7. I give advice too soon...

- Consider that the other person may primarily need to be heard and understood.

- Ask open-ended questions that encourage the other person to offer ideas.

- Don't be afraid of silence; it gives the other person a chance to continue, and it gives you a chance to collect your thoughts.

8. I tell people not to feel the way they do.

- Feelings are real for the people experiencing them. Don't expect people not to have them.

- Acknowledge the other person's feelings and include them in your understanding of the situation.

- Ask the other person to describe how his or her feelings affect work and relationships.

9. I sense that people seem upset after talking to me.

- Summarize the key points you heard the other person make. Ask whether that was what he or she was trying to communicate.

- Ask someone you trust to observe you during conversations with others and give you feedback.

- List two or three things that you may have done to contribute to the other person's reaction. At an opportune time, check your thinking with him or her.

10. **I tend to talk significantly more than the other person talks.**

- Apply the 80/20 rule. Do 80 percent of the listening and 20 percent of the talking.

- Periodically paraphrase what you have heard the other person say: "Let me see whether I heard you correctly..."

- Learn to bite your tongue rather than blurt out ideas about what is being said. This gives the other person a chance to continue, and it gives you a chance to collect your thoughts.

11. **I make it a point to fill any silences.**

- Ask yourself why you're uncomfortable with silence. Extroverted preferences? Desire to appear decisive?

- Admit your discomfort with silence to the other person: "I feel the urge to respond immediately, but I want to hear as much as possible from you."

12. I am uncomfortable when the other person expresses emotions.

- Remember that emotions can provide important data. They can tell you something about what's behind what the other person is saying.

- Name the emotions as you notice them: "You seem worried about....Tell me more about it."

- Pay attention to tone of voice, body language, and the use of specific words—both the other person's and your own—while responding to what you hear.

13. I have a hard time understanding what people are trying to say.

- Use open-ended, clarifying, and probing questions.

- Ask people to give you the essence of what they're trying to say. Repeat what you hear, and invite corrections and additions.

- If others are present, ask someone else to state what he or she heard.

Create Listening Reminders

Create active listening reminders for yourself. For example, you can copy the "Active Listening Skill Set" graphic and tape it to your computer. Print the graphic in a smaller size that you can carry with you in your wallet, keep in a notebook, or store on your smartphone. Draw or find your own image of what active listening means to you. Or reverse the approach—find an image of what poor listening can do, and use that as your reminder. Some leaders we have worked with simply write LISTEN at the top of their notes at each meeting.

Remind yourself of specific active listening behaviors and give yourself a cue or reminder to practice them. If you're honing your clarifying skills, for example, refer to a list of open-ended, clarifying, and probing questions that you've brought with you.

When possible, plan ahead for a discussion or meeting and work out your active listening strategy ahead of time just as you would think through the goals of the meeting. How will active listening help you achieve those goals? Map out specific behaviors, questions, and ideas so you will have reminders during the meeting.

14. I avoid asking any questions that would encourage the other person to talk more.

- Be clear about why you are having a conversation. Almost any valid reason requires you to ask questions and allow the other person to talk.

- Practice using incisive questions. When dealing with a long-winded person, try to discern the types of questions that help them to stay on task rather than encourage them to digress.

- Suggest a time and place for the conversation where you can be relaxed and unhurried.

15. I ask questions for which I already have the answers.

- Avoid doing this. Such an approach isn't appropriate for active listening.

- Consider that doing this may make the other person feel manipulated.

- If you have a possible answer, offer it and encourage the other person to reflect on its potential strengths and shortcomings.

16. I expect yes or no answers.

- Remind yourself that such an expectation is not appropriate for active listening.

- Review the information in this book about open-ended, clarifying, and probing questions.

- Avoid dead-end questions that ask for confirmation instead of insight: "Don't you think that...?"

17. I frequently lose track of where the conversation is going.

- Periodically paraphrase what you have heard the other person say: "Let me see whether I heard you correctly..."

- If you do lose track, ask for help: "I don't follow. Will you help me see where this is going?"

- Remind yourself of the original purpose of the conversation.

18. **I have a hard time remembering what has been said.**

- With permission from the other person, take notes to help you remember important points.

- At the end of the conversation, summarize the key points and ask for verification. Or ask the other person to summarize.

- If the conversation is important enough and both of you are comfortable with having it recorded, do so.

19. **I frequently discover that things...don't get done.**

- Toward the end of the conversation, state what you and the other person are committing to do—and by when.

- Ask the other person to send you a brief written summary of his or her agreed-upon actions.

- Consider that cultural dynamics may be at play, and follow up as needed.

20. I avoid repeating things or letting the other person repeat things.

- Remind yourself that repetition helps ensure that you understand what the other person means to say.

- Periodically ask each other what you have heard the other say to catch any miscommunication early.

- If others are present, ask someone else to state what he or she heard.

21. I keep my thoughts to myself.

- Being an active listener includes sharing your thoughts. Just remember that your primary objective is to understand; being understood is secondary.

- Build on what the other person says: "That triggered the following thought for me."

- Give the other person the first chance to express his or her thoughts during the conversation. Sharing your thoughts first may squelch the other person's ideas.

22. I keep my feelings to myself.

- Being an active listener includes sharing your feelings. By sharing them, at a level comfortable to you, you can convey empathy and active engagement.

- Use CCL's SBI (Situation, Behavior, Impact) Feedback technique described in the book *Feedback That Works: How to Build and Deliver Your Message (2nd ed.)*. Describe the situation in which the other person's behavior occurred, describe the behavior, and explain the impact that it had on you.

- Given that few of us can conceal our feelings, it makes sense to share them and, by naming them, to gain control over them.

23. I avoid sharing personal experiences.

- Remember that they are potentially tremendous sources for teaching and connecting with the other person.

- Start off with someone you trust and with relatively safe topics.

- Avoid sharing personal experiences to lecture or to diminish the other person's experience.

24. **I try hard not to let the other person know how his or her behavior affects me.**

- Do the opposite. If the behavior is inappropriate, it gives the person an opportunity to correct it or to apologize and explain.

- Use CCL's SBI Feedback technique. Describe the situation in which the other person's behavior occurred, describe the behavior, and explain the impact that it had on you.

- Invite the other person to let you know how your behavior affects him or her.

LEADING WITH ACTIVE LISTENING

Remember Maria, the leader who's having trouble with several of her direct reports? With active listening skills and a chance to go back in time, her talk with Jim could go something like this:

MARIA (entering Jim's office): Hi, Jim. Are we still good for that chat we'd scheduled?

JIM: Just one second (typing furiously to finish an email, then swiveling in his chair to face her). There. I'm ready.

MARIA (settling herself in an empty chair): Great. Thanks for taking a few minutes to talk to me—I really appreciate it. I've been sensing some tension among the members of the team, like something isn't working as well as it should (Jim's eyes take on a steely, almost guarded look), and I really wanted to get your perspective on what might be causing it and how to fix it.

JIM (organizing his thoughts and searching for words): Well . . . I feel like if there were a bit more, um, flexibility—I think that would make a difference.

MARIA (looking a little surprised): Flexibility? What do you mean?

JIM: Like, in our schedules—say, to take a shorter lunch, and then leave a little earlier in the evening.

MARIA (still clearly feeling confused): Oh... okay. Can you help me understand a little better how that can help the tension thing?

JIM: Right, yeah. So, in my case, I have to get to my son's day care after work no later than 5:20; otherwise the day care providers end up angry—and they charge a dollar every minute I'm late. If my work runs over at all and traffic isn't perfect, it gets super stressful. So I'm watching the clock constantly to get out right on time. And it basically kills the last hour and a half of my productivity.

MARIA (looking a little shocked to hear about a day care charging a dollar a minute for late pickup): Okay, that makes sense. So, if I've got this right: It's stressful to have to worry about racking up day care fees and ruffling feathers with the providers, and it eats into your productivity before you leave? And a few extra minutes would make a big difference? (Jim, no longer looking guarded, nods his head as though his voice has momentarily failed him.)

MARIA (noticing the pause): Is there more to that?

JIM (hesitating a moment before deciding to speak): Just that my son... a couple of times when work has run over, he's been the last one there. And he told me... (Jim's voice catches briefly) he told me he was worried I just wasn't going to come back for him at all. (Quickly regaining his composure) Sorry—I don't mean to be unprofessional.

MARIA: No worries. It sounds like this is really hard on you. I don't have kids of my own, so I haven't experienced that feeling myself. But I understand how that few minutes could be really valuable to your family.

JIM: And it wouldn't need to be a lot more time, either.

MARIA: So, if you could shift your workday to have a hard stop, say, 20 minutes before 5:00, do you feel like it would improve your focus during the rest of the afternoon?

JIM (with a curt nod of his head): Yes—and I know there are a few other parents on the team who are in the same boat as me.

MARIA (pulling a notepad from her pocket and pausing to jot something down before looking up): Okay, Jim, wow—this is really helpful information. I can't make any promises yet—I need to talk to the other members of the team and get their perspectives, too, before I'll really understand my options. But I really appreciate your taking the time to talk to me.

MARIA (after a brief pause to see if Jim has more to say): Well, Jim, I'm glad we had this chance to talk. Like I said, I need to get everyone else's perspective, too, but this is all really valuable. In the meantime, if you have any other thoughts, would you shoot me an email or just drop by my office? The door's always open.

JIM: I will, thanks!

Active listening can make a huge difference in our interactions with others. Working relationships become more solid, based on trust, respect, and honesty. Leaders benefit from the depth of engagement and information that can come as a result—it lets them plan and proceed with greater insight and knowledge. Active listening is not an optional component of leadership; it is not a nicety to be used to make others feel good. It is, in fact, a critical component of the tasks facing today's leaders.

Suggested Resources

Barker, L. L., & Watson, K. W. (2000). *Listen up: How to improve relationships, reduce stress, and be more productive by using the power of listening.* New York, NY: St. Martin's Press.

Center for Creative Leadership (2018). *Better conversations every day.* Greensboro, NC: Center for Creative Leadership. https://www.ccl.org/leadership-solutions/coaching-services/better-conversations-every-day/

Center for Creative Leadership (2019). *Feedback that works: How to build and deliver your message* (2nd ed.) Greensboro, NC: Center for Creative Leadership.

Kiewitz, C., Weaver, J. B., Hans-Bernd, B., & Weimann, G. (1997). Cultural differences in listening style preferences: A comparison of young adults in Germany, Israel, and the United States. *International Journal of Public Opinion Research, 9*(3), 233-247.

Samovar, L. A., Porter, R. E., McDaniel, E. R., & Roy, C. S. (2016). *Communication between cultures* (9th ed.). Boston, MA: Cengage Learning.

Scisco, P., Biech, E., & Hallenbeck, G. (2017). *Compass: Your guide for leadership development and coaching.* Greensboro, NC: Center for Creative Leadership.

Shafir, R. Z. (2003). *The Zen of listening: Mindful communication in the age of distraction.* Wheaton, IL: Quest Books.

Sullivan, J. E. (2000). *The good listener.* Notre Dame, IN: Ave Maria Press.

Background

Since 1970, CCL has worked with thousands of leaders to develop their skills, following a process of using heightened self-awareness to help these leaders adapt and grow their skill set. As such, active listening is a core tool embedded throughout our programs and the assessments we use.

While active listening has long been recognized in industry as a useful leadership and development technique, we've come to see it as a skill set core to all effective leaders, particularly amid the heightened demands of an increasingly diverse and interconnected world. Skills indispensable to effective leadership—the ability to adapt and remain flexible in the face of change, take the perspective of others, lead employees with a participative management style, build and mend relationships, and manage change—all rest on the fundamental bedrock of the ability to listen. It is our experience that those leaders who struggle most can trace those difficulties to deficits in active listening skills, and that even small improvements in active listening can quickly return large yields in career outcomes.

Active listening also undergirds our feedback and coaching methodology. We practice what we preach: To work with a coachee effectively, the Center requires that each coach be a skilled practitioner of active listening.

It is our desire to increase awareness and mastery of this much-neglected but increasingly crucial art that has led to the publication of this book.

LIMITED-TIME OFFER!

Discount off your next workshop kit purchase
Visit: ccl.org/listenpromo

Listen to Understand Workshop Kit

High achievers know how to develop trust and relationships with others using the power of listening. CCL's *Listen to Understand* workshop provides tools and skills to make it easier to learn and practice effective listening. By learning specifically what to do (or avoid doing) to be a better listener, leaders encounter fewer misunderstandings, resolve more conflicts, and waste less time.

Additional Resources for Communication:

A Better Culture Starts with Better Conversations
Coaching Skills for Every Employee
ccl.org/bce

Better Conversations Every Day (BCE) is a one-day experience that provides coaching skills across an entire organization. BCE will help an organization:

- *Act with greater agility and resilience*
- *Address issues with openness and respect*
- *Engage effectively in ongoing performance discussions*
- *Create a culture of honest feedback and continual coaching*